HAL·LEONARD

PIANO PLAY-ALONG

LOVE SONGS

T0052939

ISBN 0-634-06907-1

HAL·LEONARD®
CORPORATION

7777 W. BLUEMOUND RD. P.O. BOX 13819 MILWAUKEE, WI 53213

Visit Hal Leonard Online at
www.halleonard.com

CONTENTS

CAN'T HELP FALLING IN LOVE

from the Paramount Picture BLUE HAWAII

Words and Music by GEORGE DAVID WEISS,
HUGO PERETTI and LUIGI CREATORE

Slowly, steadily

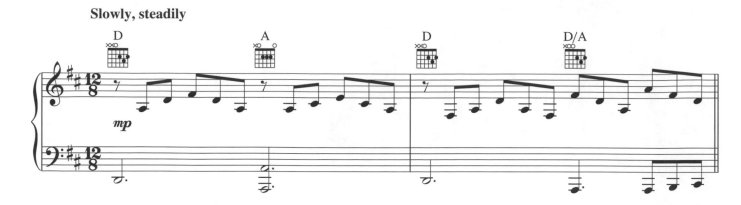

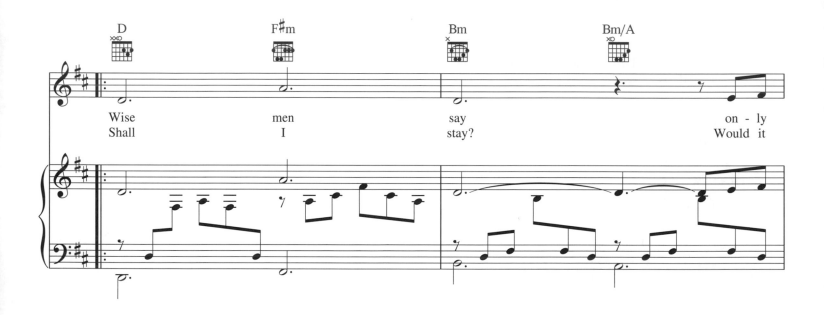

Wise   men   say   on - ly
Shall   I   stay?   Would it

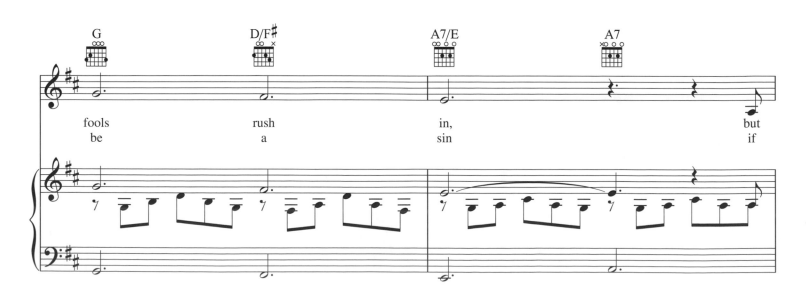

fools   rush   in,   but
be   a   sin   if

(They Long to Be)
CLOSE TO YOU

Lyric by HAL DAVID
Music by BURT BACHARACH

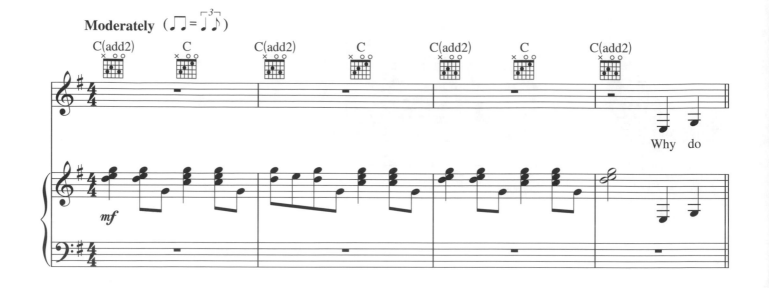

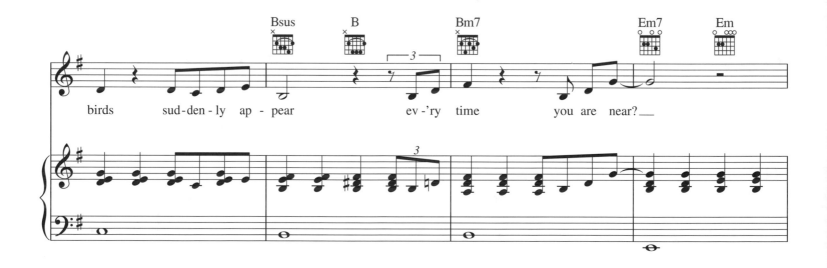

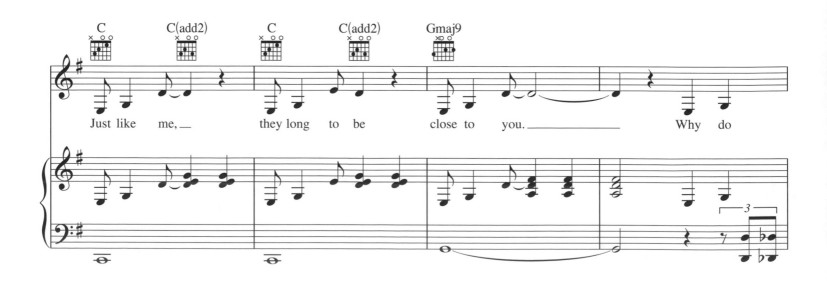

HERE, THERE AND EVERYWHERE

Words and Music by JOHN LENNON
and PAUL McCARTNEY

HOW DEEP IS YOUR LOVE

from the Motion Picture SATURDAY NIGHT FEVER

Words and Music by ROBIN GIBB,
MAURICE GIBB and BARRY GIBB

I HONESTLY LOVE YOU

Words and Music by PETER ALLEN
and JEFF BARRY

WONDERFUL TONIGHT

Words and Music by
ERIC CLAPTON

It's late in the eve - ning;
We go to a par - ty,
It's time to go home ___ now,

she's won - d'ring what clothes ___ to wear. ___
and ev - 'ry - one turns ___ to see ___
and I've got an ach - ing head. ___

She puts on her make -
this beau - ti - ful la -
So I give her the car ___

D.S. al Coda

YOU ARE SO BEAUTIFUL

Words and Music by BILLY PRESTON
and BRUCE FISHER

Moderately slow, expressively

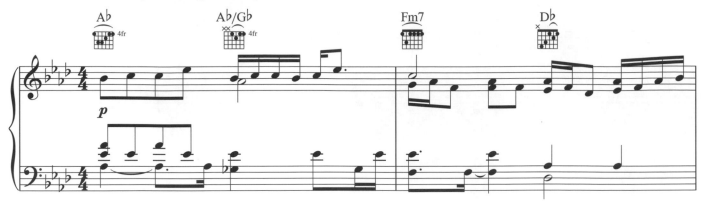

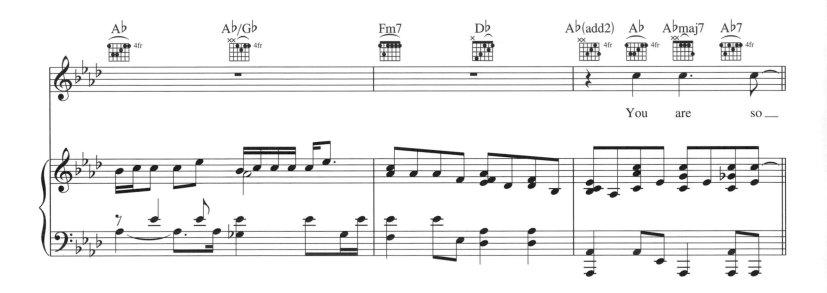

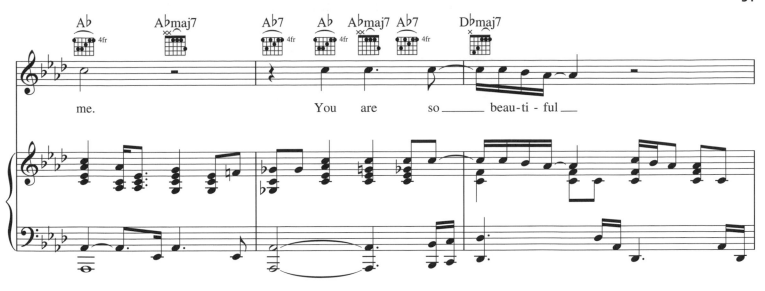

me. You are so ___ beau-ti - ful ___

to me. Can't you

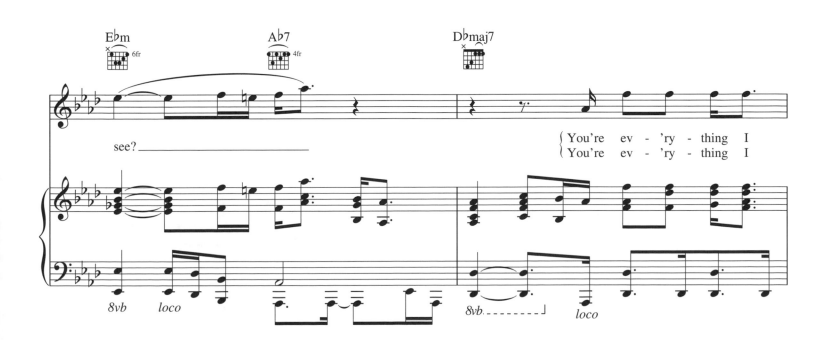

see? ___

You're ev -'ry - thing I
You're ev -'ry - thing I

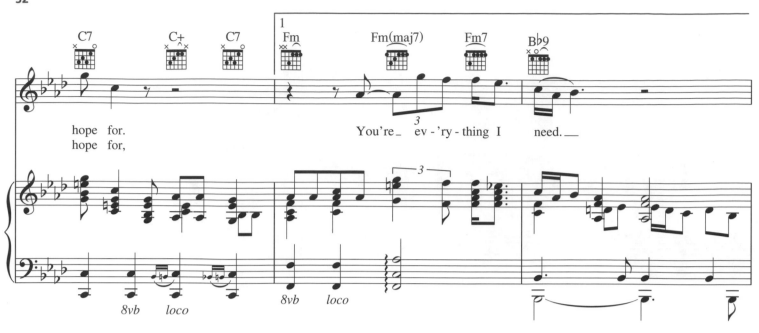

hope for.
hope for,

You're ev-'ry-thing I need.

You are so beau-ti-ful to me.

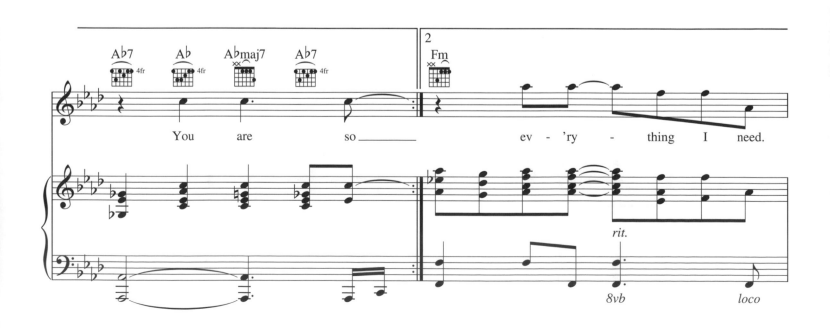

You are so ev-'ry-thing I need.

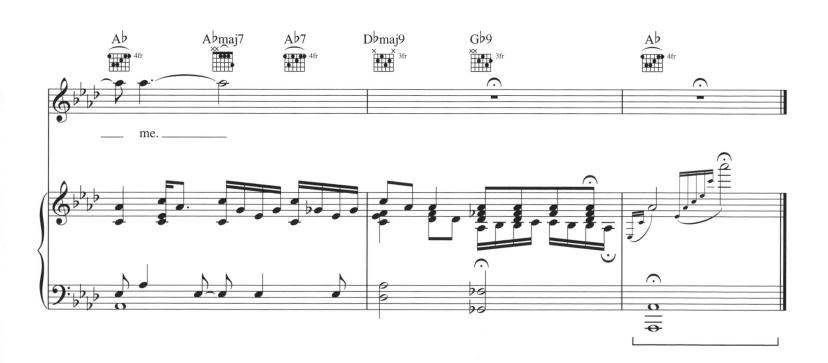

MAYBE I'M AMAZED

Words and Music by
PAUL McCARTNEY

1. Ba - by, I'm a - mazed at the way you love me all the time, ___
2. *Instrumental*
3. May - be I'm a - mazed at the way you're with me all the time, ___
4. *Instrumental*

and may - be I'm a - fraid of the way I love you. ___

and may - be I'm a - fraid of the way I need you. ___

The Most Romantic Music In The World

Arranged for piano, voice, and guitar

The Best Love Songs Ever – 2nd Edition

This revised edition includes 65 romantic favorites: Always • Beautiful in My Eyes • Can You Feel the Love Tonight • Endless Love • Have I Told You Lately • Misty • Something • Through the Years • Truly • When I Fall in Love • and more.

00359198 ....$19.95

The Big Book of Love Songs – 2nd Edition

80 romantic hits in many musical styles: Always on My Mind • Cherish • Fields of Gold • I Honestly Love You • I'll Be There • Isn't It Romantic? • Lady • My Heart Will Go On • Save the Best for Last • Truly • Wonderful Tonight • and more.

00310784 ....$19.95

The Christian Wedding Songbook

37 songs of love and commitment, including: Bonded Together • Cherish the Treasure • Flesh of My Flesh • Go There with You • Household of Faith • How Beautiful • I Will Be Here • Love Will Be Our Home • Make Us One • Parent's Prayer • This Is the Day • This Very Day • and more.

00310681 ....$16.95

The Bride's Guide to Wedding Music

This great guide is a complete resource for planning wedding music. It includes a thorough article on choosing music for a wedding ceremony, and 65 songs in many different styles to satisfy lots of different tastes. The songs are grouped by categories, including preludes, processionals, recessionals, traditional sacred songs, popular songs, country songs, contemporary Christian songs, Broadway numbers, and new age piano music.

00310615 ....$19.95

Broadway Love Songs

50 romantic favorites from shows such as *Phantom of the Opera*, *Guys and Dolls*, *Oklahoma!*, *South Pacific*, *Fiddler on the Roof* and more. Songs include: All I Ask of You • Bewitched • I've Grown Accustomed to Her Face • Love Changes Everything • So in Love • Sunrise, Sunset • Unexpected Song • We Kiss in a Shadow • and more.

00311558 ....$15.95

Country Love Songs – 4th Edition

This edition features 34 romantic country favorites: Amazed • Breathe • Could I Have This Dance • Forever and Ever, Amen • I Need You • The Keeper of the Stars • Love Can Build a Bridge • One Boy, One Girl • Stand by Me • This Kiss • Through the Years • Valentine • You Needed Me • more.

00311528 ....$14.95

The Definitive Love Collection – 2nd Edition

100 romantic favorites – all in one convenient collection! Includes: All I Ask of You • Can't Help Falling in Love • Endless Love • The Glory of Love • Have I Told You Lately • Heart and Soul • Lady in Red • Love Me Tender • My Romance • So in Love • Somewhere Out There • Unforgettable • Up Where We Belong • When I Fall in Love • and more!

00311681 ....$24.95

I Will Be Here

Over two dozen romantic selections from top contemporary Christian artists such as Susan Ashton, Avalon, Steven Curtis Chapman, Twila Paris, Sonicflood, and others. Songs include: Answered Prayer • Beautiful in My Eyes • Celebrate You • For Always • Give Me Forever (I Do) • Go There with You • How Beautiful • Love Will Be Our Home • and more.

00306472 ....$17.95

Love Songs

Budget Books Series

74 favorite love songs, including: And I Love Her • Cherish • Crazy • Endless Love • Fields of Gold • I Just Called to Say I Love You • I'll Be There • (You Make Me Feel Like) A Natural Woman • Wonderful Tonight • You Are So Beautiful • and more.

00310834 ....$12.95

The New Complete Wedding Songbook

41 of the most requested and beloved songs for romance and weddings: Anniversary Song • Ave Maria • Canon in D (Pachelbel) • Could I Have This Dance • Endless Love • I Love You Truly • Just the Way You Are • The Lord's Prayer • Through the Years • You Needed Me • Your Song • and more.

00309326 ....$12.95

New Ultimate Love and Wedding Songbook

This whopping songbook features 90 songs of devotion, including: The Anniversary Waltz • Can't Smile Without You • Could I Have This Dance • Endless Love • For All We Know • Forever and Ever, Amen • The Hawaiian Wedding Song • Here, There and Everywhere • I Only Have Eyes for You • Just the Way You Are • Longer • The Lord's Prayer • Love Me Tender • Misty • Somewhere • Sunrise, Sunset • Through the Years • Trumpet Voluntary • Your Song • and more.

00361445 ....$19.95

Romance – Boleros Favoritos

Features 48 Spanish and Latin American favorites: Aquellos Ojos Verdes • Bésame Mucho • El Reloj • Frenes • Inolvidable • La Vida Es Un Sueño • Perfidia • Siempre En Mi Corazón • Solamente Una Vez • more.

00310383 ....$16.95

Soulful Love Songs

Features 35 favorite romantic ballads, including: All My Life • Baby, Come to Me • Being with You • Endless Love • Hero • I Just Called to Say I Love You • I'll Make Love to You • I'm Still in Love with You • Killing Me Softly with His Song • My Cherie Amour • My Eyes Adored You • Oh Girl • On the Wings of Love • Overjoyed • Tonight, I Celebrate My Love • Vision of Love • You Are the Sunshine of My Life • You've Made Me So Very Happy • and more.

00310922 ....$14.95

Selections from VH1's 100 Greatest Love Songs

Nearly 100 love songs chosen for their emotion. Includes: Always on My Mind • Baby, I Love Your Way • Careless Whisper • Endless Love • How Deep Is Your Love • I Got You Babe • If You Leave Me Now • Love Me Tender • My Heart Will Go On • Unchained Melody • You're Still the One • and dozens more!

00306506 ....$27.95

FOR MORE INFORMATION, SEE YOUR LOCAL MUSIC DEALER, OR WRITE TO:

HAL•LEONARD® CORPORATION

7777 W. BLUEMOUND RD. P.O. BOX 13819 MILWAUKEE, WI 53213

www.halleonard.com

1004

THE DEFINITIVE COLLECTIONS

These magnificent folios each feature a quintessential selection of songs. Each has outstanding piano/vocal arrangements showcased by beautiful full-color covers. Books are spiral-bound for convenience and longevity.

The Definitive Blues Collection

A massive collection of 96 blues classics. Songs include: Baby, Won't You Please Come Home • Basin Street Blues • Everyday (I Have the Blues) • Gloomy Sunday • I'm a Man • (I'm Your) Hoochie Coochie Man • Milk Cow Blues • Nobody Knows You When You're Down and Out • The Seventh Son • St. Louis Blues • The Thrill Is Gone • and more.
00311563 ....$24.95

The Definitive Country Collection

A must-own collection of 101 country classics, including: Coward of the County • Crazy • Forever and Ever, Amen • Friends in Low Places • Grandpa (Tell Me About the Good Old Days) • Help Me Make It Through the Night • Make the World Go Away • Mammas Don't Let Your Babies Grow Up to Be Cowboys • Okie from Muskogee • Through the Years • and many more.
00311555 ....$24.95

The Definitive Jazz Collection

88 of the greatest jazz songs ever, including: Ain't Misbehavin' • All the Things You Are • Birdland • Body and Soul • The Girl from Ipanema • The Lady Is a Tramp • Midnight Sun • Moonlight in Vermont • Night and Day • Skylark • Stormy Weather • Sweet Georgia Brown • and more.
00359571 ....$24.95

The Definitive Broadway Collection

121 of the greatest show tunes ever compiled into one volume, including: All I Ask of You • And All That Jazz • Don't Cry for Me Argentina • Hello, Dolly! • I Could Have Danced All Night • I Dreamed a Dream • Memory • Some Enchanted Evening • The Sound of Music • The Surrey with the Fringe on Top • Tomorrow • What I Did for Love • more.
00359570 ....$24.95

The Definitive Dixieland Collection

73 Dixieland classics, including: Ain't Misbehavin' • Alexander's Ragtime Band • Basin Street Blues • Bill Bailey, Won't You Please Come Home? • Dinah • Do You Know What It Means to Miss New Orleans? • I Ain't Got Nobody • King Porter Stomp • Maple Leaf Rag • Original Dixieland One-Step • When the Saints Go Marching In • and more.
00311575 ....$24.95

The Definitive Love Collection

100 sentimental favorites! Includes: All I Ask of You • Can't Help Falling in Love • Endless Love • The Glory of Love • I've Got My Love to Keep Me Warm • Isn't It Romantic? • Love Me Tender • Save the Best for Last • So in Love • Somewhere Out There • Unforgettable • When I Fall in Love • You Are So Beautiful • more.
00311681 ....$24.95

The Definitive Christmas Collection

An authoritative collection of 127 Christmas classics, including: Blue Christmas • The Chipmunk Song • The Christmas Song (Chestnuts Roasting) • Feliz Navidad • Frosty the Snow Man • Happy Hanukkah, My Friend • Happy Holiday • (There's No Place Like) Home for the Holidays • O Come, All Ye Faithful • Rudolph, the Red-Nosed Reindeer • Tennessee Christmas • more!
00311602 ....$24.95

The Definitive Hymn Collection

An amazing collection of 218 treasured hymns, including: Abide with Me • All Glory, Laud and Honor • All Things Bright and Beautiful • At the Cross • Battle Hymn of the Republic • Be Thou My Vision • Blessed Assurance • Church in the Wildwood • Higher Ground • How Firm a Foundation • In the Garden • Just As I Am • A Mighty Fortress Is Our God • Nearer, My God, to Thee • The Old Rugged Cross • Rock of Ages • Sweet By and By • Were You There? • and more.
00310773 ....$24.95

The Definitive Movie Collection

A comprehensive collection of 105 songs that set the moods for movies, including: Alfie • Beauty and the Beast • Blue Velvet • Can You Feel the Love Tonight • Easter Parade • Endless Love • Forrest Gump Suite • Theme from Jurassic Park • My Heart Will Go On • The Rainbow Connection • Someday My Prince Will Come • Under the Sea • Up Where We Belong • and more.
00311705 ....$29.95

The Definitive Classical Collection

129 favorite classical piano pieces and instrumental and operatic literature transcribed for piano. Features music by Johann Sebastian Bach, Ludwig van Beethoven, Georges Bizet, Johannes Brahms, Frederic Chopin, Claude Debussy, George Frideric Handel, Felix Mendelssohn, Johann Pachelbel, Franz Schubert, Johann Strauss, Jr., Pyotr Il'yich Tchaikovsky, Richard Wagner, and many more!
00310772 ....$29.95

The Definitive Rock 'n' Roll Collection

A classic collection of the best songs from the early rock 'n' roll years: 1955-1968. 95 songs, including: Barbara Ann • Chantilly Lace • Dream Lover • Duke of Earl • Earth Angel • Great Balls of Fire • Louie, Louie • Rock Around the Clock • Ruby Baby • Runaway • (Seven Little Girls) Sitting in the Back Seat • Stay • Surfin' U.S.A. • Wild Thing • Woolly Bully • and more.
00490195 ....$24.95

Prices, contents and availability subject to change without notice.

FOR MORE INFORMATION, SEE YOUR LOCAL MUSIC DEALER, OR WRITE TO:

HAL•LEONARD®
CORPORATION

7777 W. BLUEMOUND RD. P.O. BOX 13819 MILWAUKEE, WI 53213

www.halleonard.com

0306